Preface

If you've read much about Zen Buddhism, you're probably aware of its "public cases" (Japanese, *koans*)—strange but wonderful stories about masters, monks, and enlightenment. Here is an example:

> The emperor asked Zen Master Gudo, "What happens to an enlightened being after death?"
>
> "How should I know?" replied the master.
>
> "Because you are an enlightened being," answered the emperor.
>
> "Yes," the master said, "but not a dead one."

In that spirit, here are tales not of the Zen master but rather of the Pen master, whose job is to open the minds of editors everywhere. As is customary in Zen tradition, each story is followed by enlightening commentary.

Like Zen koans, these stories are meant to be contemplated. I hope the stories are entertaining, but they shouldn't be just chomped down like pieces of popcorn. Take time to ponder each one, and you may yet become enlightened in the pathways of publishing.

Tales of the Pen Master

Tales of the Pen Master

*Zen Stories for Editors, Writers,
and Other Publishing Professionals*

Jack Lyon

THE EDITORIUM

ISBN 978-1-4341-0430-4

The Editorium™ is a trademark of The Editorium, LLC
West Jordan, UT 84081-6132
www.editorium.com

Contents

Rules

An assistant editor went before the Pen master, saying, "Lo, these many years I have faithfully followed the precepts in *Garner's Modern American Usage* and *The Chicago Manual of Style*. Why am I not yet enlightened?"

"Because," said the master, "you have faithfully followed the precepts in *Garner's Modern American Usage* and *The Chicago Manual of Style*."

In true Zen spirit, this story illustrates the importance of following the rules and *not* following the rules. Editors have "rules" for an important reason—to make sure the author's intended meaning is clearly communicated to readers in a consistent, coherent way. But blindly following the "rules" can also result in miscommunication. That is why, since its initial publication in 1906, *The Chicago Manual of Style* has included the following disclaimer: "Rules and regulations such as these, in the nature of the case, cannot be endowed with the fixity of rock-ribbed law. They are meant for the average case, and must be applied with a certain degree of elasticity."

Mechanics

One day the Pen master was passing an assistant's cubicle.

"Oh, master," said the assistant, "I'm so glad you came by. Look at this wonderful new editing software. It flags incomplete sentences, finds dangling modifiers, and much more. With this software, the manuscript practically edits itself!"

"Interesting," said the master. "How does it know when a paragraph should be deleted?"

Editing is not simply a matter of mechanics; if it were, a computer could do it. Fortunately for editors, a human mind is required. At the Editorium (www.editorium.com) I create and sell Microsoft Word add-ins to help editors do their work. These add-ins, to some degree, automate parts of the editing process. But in the end, cognitive judgment is needed to decide which parts should be automated and which should not, and if any of the automated parts should in some cases be overridden. In addition, there are many parts of the process that simply cannot be automated. Language is complex and subtle, and something as small as a misplaced decimal point (in a medical journal, for example) can literally make the difference between life and death.

Meaning

After receiving his edited manuscript for review, the author was furious. "How dare you!" he said to the Pen master. "This manuscript is covered with corrections."

"You must not look at the corrections," said the master. "You must look at the meaning behind the corrections."

Editing is not about making corrections. Rather, it is about making sure the author's writing is clear—and not just to the reader. An editor is not out of place to say to an author, "You seem to be saying *this,* but what I think you really mean is *this.* Is that right?" It's all about *meaning.*

It is *not* the editor's place, however, to *add* meaning, to "improve" the author's ideas. Editors who feel the need to do so should write their own books.

If It Ain't Broke, Don't Fix It

An assistant editor came to the Pen master. "Here is the manuscript I have been editing. I have meticulously improved anything that could be improved." The assistant made a deep bow. "My work is finished.

"Excellent," said the master. "Thank you for your careful attention."

After the assistant had departed, the master looked through the manuscript and stetted many of the assistant's changes.

"Now that's what I call finished," he said.

Just because editors *can* improve something doesn't mean they *should*. Is the text clear as it stands? Then leave it alone! Why do you feel the need to do otherwise?

Consider the *bonsai,* the beautiful miniature tree whose cultivation originated in China, then spread eastward to Korea and Japan. The gardener's job is not to force the tree into some "correct" position but rather to enhance the tree's natural shape, to fully reveal the tree's inherent beauty. The editor's job is similar.

The principle is illustrated in a story about the great Japanese tea-master Sen no Rikyu:

> Rikyu was watching his son Shoan as he swept and watered the garden path. "Not clean enough," said Rikyu, when Shoan had finished his task, and bade him try again. After a weary hour the son turned to Rikyu: "Father, there is nothing more to be done. The steps have been washed for the third time, the stone lanterns and the trees are well sprinkled with water, moss and lichens are shining with a fresh verdure; not a twig, not a leaf have I left on the ground." "Young fool," chided the tea-master, "that is not the way a garden path should be swept." Saying this, Rikyu stepped into the garden, shook a tree and scattered over the garden gold and crimson leaves, scraps of the brocade of autumn! What Rikyu demanded was not cleanliness alone, but the beautiful and the natural also. (Kakuzo Okakura, *The Book of Tea* [Tokyo: Kodansha International, 1989], 84.)

Of course an editor should make sure that a manuscript is as clean and consistent as possible. But if readers can *tell* that the book has been edited—if the editing is actually noticeable—the editor has failed. Done correctly, editing is invisible, and a well-edited text reads as naturally as leaves fall in the garden.

An assistant editor was reading a manuscript that had already been gone over by the Pen master. To her surprise, the manuscript contained not a single correction.

Questioning the master about this, the assistant remarked, "You said you had edited this manuscript, but it contains no corrections at all."

"Nevertheless," said the master, "now that I'm finished with it, the manuscript is perfect."

What if you went completely through a manuscript without making a single correction, because, as far as you could tell, no corrections were needed? Would you have done your job? I believe that you would have. An editor's job is not to make corrections; an editor's job is to make sure the writing is clear, and if it is, no corrections are needed. Of course, in real life, that is probably never the case. But it's an interesting thing to think about.

Something Is Always Broke

An assistant brought a new book, hot off the press, to the Pen master. "Master, look!" she said. "The book is beautiful! The cover is bright and attractive, the marketing copy is appealing, the typography is excellent. Surely this is the finest book we have ever published."

The master opened the book to a random page. "Read the first line," he said.

"'When this came to the attention of the pubic ...'"

These are the things that haunt our lives. I started my publishing career as a proofreader at a university press. On prominent display in our office was a book on whose cover the title had been misspelled—a reminder of the need for constant vigilance on *every part* of the book during *every part* of the publishing process. At a later job, thousands of copies of a publication ended up being shredded because of a photograph that should not have been included. So pay attention! As a famous Zen story teaches:

A student said to Master Ichu, "Please write for me something of great wisdom."

Master Ichu picked up his brush and wrote one word: "Attention."

ちゅうもく

The student said, "Is that all?"

The master wrote, "Attention. Attention."

The student became irritable. "That doesn't seem profound or subtle to me."

In response, Master Ichu wrote simply, "Attention. Attention. Attention."

In frustration, the student demanded, "What does this word *attention* mean?"

Master Ichu replied, "Attention means attention."

(Charlotte Joko Beck, *Nothing Special: Living Zen.* [New York: HarperCollins, 1993], 168.)

Context

An editor and a designer were arguing about which was more important, layout or words.

"The layout is finished," said the designer. "You'll need to edit the wording to fit."

"The editing is finished," said the editor. "You'll need to change the design to accommodate."

Around and around they went. Finally, they took their argument before the Pen master, who looked at them severely. "What matters is neither the design nor the words," he said. "What matters is the meaning."

"And how does one know the meaning?" asked the editor.

"By looking at the design and the words."

This is what makes publishing so interesting—and so difficult. The meaning of a word or a sentence or a paragraph always depends on what's going on around it. Ideas are not fixed; as we change the words or design of a publication, meanings change too, so we must be constantly on our guard.

A student once asked Zen master Shunryu Suzuki, "Can you reduce Buddhism to one phrase?" His reply was instantaneous and profound: "Everything changes." (David Chadwick, *Crooked Cucumber: The Life and Zen Teachings of Shunryu Suzuki* [New York: Broadway Books, 1999], xii.)

Another Pen master story illustrates the same principle:

One day an assistant came to the Pen master for help with an awkward sentence.

"No matter what I do, I can't seem to fix this sentence," he said. "If I delete a word, the sentence no longer makes sense. If I add a word, the sentence seems bloated."

"If fixing the sentence doesn't fix it," the master replied, "perhaps it doesn't need fixing."

The next day, the assistant came to the Pen master for help with another awkward sentence.

"Again," he said, "I can't seem to fix this sentence. If I delete a word, the sentence no longer makes sense. If I add a word, the sentence seems bloated."

The master picked up his pen and deleted the sentence entirely. "There," he said. "Now the fixing is fixed."

After a sleepless night, the assistant came again to the Pen master.

"The first day, you said the sentence didn't need fixing. The second day, you simply deleted the sentence. How does one know when to fix and when to delete?"

The master looked at him shrewdly. "It doesn't depend on the sentence; it depends on the sentences around it."

Thinking to outwit the master, the assistant replied,

"And what if there are no sentences around it? Then how does one know what to do?"

The master gave a great sigh. "One doesn't," he said.

Taste

An assistant came to the Pen master for advice about rec-
onciling proofs.

"One proofreader fixes an error one way; another fixes
another way," said the assistant. "Which is right?"

"Neither is right; neither is wrong," said the master.
"What matters is that the error was fixed."

The "Vinegar Tasters," often depicted in Asian art, represent
the founders of the three Eastern religious traditions: Buddhism,
Confucianism, and Taoism. The three sages dip their fingers into
a vat of vinegar and taste it. Buddha finds it bitter, like the suf-
fering of humanity. Confucius deems it sour, like the corruption
of society. To Lao Tzu, the vinegar is simply delicious, like life
itself, whatever its flavor may be.

Editors sometimes argue about the "right" way to make a correction, but their different points of view may just be a matter of
taste. How something is fixed may be irrelevant as long as the
meaning is clear. There are other considerations, of course, such
as elegance, euphony, and—perhaps—even beauty. But these are

in the realm of enlightenment beyond enlightenment. For now, just make sure the sweet-and-sour sauce is tasty.

Evaluation

The Pen master had rejected the manuscript, but the author insisted on meeting with him to plead her case.

"Surely my manuscript has merit," she said. "According to the sutras, all manuscripts have Book-nature."

"Yes, they do," said the master. "But not this one."

This is a take-off on the most famous and probably the shortest story in Zen literature—"Joshu's Mu." The Japanese word *mu* (the vowel sound is the same as that in *book*) means "no; not have; without." Here's the story:

A monk asked Master Joshu, "Has a dog Buddha-nature or not?"

Joshu answered, "Mu."

What makes this story interesting is that according to Buddhist teaching, *all* sentient beings have "Buddha-nature," even the dirty, smelly, mangy cur that prowls the monastery looking for something to eat. But when the monk asks about this,

Joshu repudiates that universal teaching. Or does he? Could he actually be saying something else? And if so, what is it? That question is the point of the story, which is often given to novitiates to ponder as their introduction to Zen.

The Pen master agrees that all manuscripts have "Booknature," for with thorough editing or perhaps rewriting, even the worst of manuscripts can be salvaged. Or can it? How do we know ahead of time whether our efforts will be worthwhile? What if the manuscript's content is outstanding but its writing is not? And if the writing is bad, how can we accurately judge the content? Is the worth of a manuscript determined by its content, its expression of that content, or both? What makes a manuscript worth publishing? What makes it a dog?

I once edited a book by one of the most widely known business consultants in the world; his previous books had sold millions of copies. The manuscript had been worked on by another editor, but it was still a rather disjointed pile of notes and stories. My task was to finish the organization and polish the text. The result? A masterpiece. But did the manuscript have Book-nature? And do puppies have dog-nature? What do you think?

Technology

One day an assistant came to the master in great distress. "My computer has stopped working, and the IT guy is at lunch. How am I supposed to work?"

The master spoke not a word but held up a red pen.

Technology is both wonderful and terrible—wonderful when it works, and terrible when it doesn't. Even when it works, it's valuable to know how things were done before the advent of the computer. After all, monks in the scriptorium, working with pen and ink on parchment, still managed to churn out thousands of books, and the processes they developed continue to inform our work today, even though we may not realize it.

I once edited a book about a man who had been the personal secretary to the president of a large corporation back in the 1940s, hired primarily because he knew how to take dictation in shorthand. At an important meeting, he decided to abandon his shorthand notes and capture the proceedings with a newly developed recording machine made for use in court. After the meeting, the president approached him. "Well," he said, "did I speak too fast for you tonight?"

"No, I got along just fine," the clueless secretary replied. "I used a machine to record everything, so I didn't need to fuss with shorthand."

"Yes, I noticed that. But what if the machine had broken? What if the electricity had gone out? I've always thought it's better to have the notes and not need them than to need them and not have them."

From then on, the secretary took everything down in shorthand, even if someone was recording the meeting electronically.

If you worked in publishing earlier than about 1985, you edited a (usually) typewritten manuscript on paper. After you finished, a typesetter retyped the entire text (including your changes) and ran out typeset galleys. Then a proofreader checked the typesetter's work against your edited manuscript. But today, after a manuscript is edited electronically, it will *not* be retyped. In fact, it will *become* the typeset galleys, which won't really be galleys at all but rather page proofs in PDF form. And if you entered the publishing field less than twenty years ago, you may not even know what galleys and page proofs are, in which case what I've just said may be meaningless to you.

Using an electronically edited manuscript for typesetting is a good thing. It completely prevents all of the errors that would be introduced if a typesetter retyped it. But it also conflates what used to be two distinct phases in the production process, eliminating the opportunity to have someone comb through the text of a book *in a different way* from what the editor has done. Comparing galley proofs and manuscript point by point forced proofreaders to read slowly, catching not only the typesetter's errors but also problems the editor may have overlooked in a straight read-through. But no more. Editing on computer may have increased our efficiency, but I sometimes wonder what it has done to our effectiveness.

One day the IT manager brought a large silver box to the publishing department and installed it in the publishing library.

"What have we here?" the Pen master asked.

"A state-of-the-art data server," the manager said. "The Corporate overlords have decreed that you will use it to store all of your work."

"Indeed we will," said the master. "Thank you very much."

A few days later, an editor knocked on the master's door. "I can't find the manuscript for the book I'm supposed to edit this week. Do you know where it might be?"

"Yes," replied the master. "You'll find it on top of the large silver box in the library."

As a software junkie, I'm always investigating the latest programs for writing, editing, and typesetting, hoping someday to find the perfect tool for all my publishing needs. But I would probably accomplish more if I stopped obsessing over this and just used the tools I have to do the work I need to do. Two of the most productive authors I know continue to write in WordPerfect 5.1. And why not? The program does everything they need, without the feature bloat we find in, say, Microsoft Word.

The fancy features promised in new software and hardware may be valuable when based on the actual needs of users rather than the heady ideas of marketing managers, but that is seldom the case. More and more, I find myself drawn to the serenity of simplicity rather than the chaos of complexity.

Sources

An assistant met with the Pen master for a status report.

"So," said the master, "you are fact-checking your current manuscript. How is that going?"

"Very well," said the assistant. "Wikipedia, especially, is a wonderful source of information."

"Yes," said the master. "But who will fact-check Wikipedia?"

Wikipedia is an easy target for ridicule. As Michael Scott says in the television series *The Office,* "Wikipedia is the best thing ever. Anyone in the world can write anything they want about any subject, so you *know* you are getting the best possible information." We laugh, but any source has its inaccuracies.

A few years ago, out of curiosity, I looked up an article in *Encyclopædia Britannica* (that trusted bastion of knowledge) on a topic with which I was intimately familiar. I knew and had actually worked with most of the experts in the field. But had any of them written the *Britannica* article? No, they had not. In fact, I'd never heard of the person who had. And to make things worse, the article was riddled with errors. So Wikipedia or *Britannica?* What makes a fact factual?

Marketing

The Pen master and an assistant were walking down the hallway when the marketing manager went by.

"There's something I've been wondering about," said the assistant. "Does a marketing manager have Book-nature?"

The master looked puzzled. "I don't know," he said.

Several years ago, American Editor Rich Adin and I had a long talk about book marketing. The conversation went like this:

Jack: I hate the whole corporate mindset that treats books as "product"—just a homogeneous mass of words and pages. It's like marketing dish soap.

Rich: That's how books *should* be marketed.

Jack: What?!

Rich: Yep. Just like dish soap. How else would you do it?

I never did come up with a good answer to that question.

As a young editor at a trade publishing house, I admired the company president, who held not an MBA but a Ph.D. in English literature. Here was an executive who actually cared about books! In a speech to employees, I heard him say this: "I love the opportunity we have to share what we do with others, to be able to face a customer and honestly say, 'I love what I'm doing, and I can share something with you that can change your life forever. I can give you a friend that will never, ever leave you.' . . .

"It was at least ten years ago that I heard Charles Scribner say, 'If books become obsolete, I will make candles.' He didn't explain his remark, but I think he had in mind that although the electric light has made candles obsolete, candlemaking today is a $100 million industry—not large, but it casts a lovely light, and, after all, books are candles."

Shortly after that speech, the chairman of the board assigned the president a new position—as CEO of a department store. This man who loved books so much ended up selling kitchen appliances and underwear.

I see the commoditization of books as analogous to the commoditization of everything else, including people. We no longer have personnel departments; instead, we have human resources. We no longer have leaders who understand a particular industry; instead, we have MBAs who are cranked out like sausages to work in any industry. With our narrow focus on the bottom line, we've ripped the heart out of our businesses—at least, those that used to have one.

So, can marketing managers have Book-nature? After all, they do sell books. But are those books commodities, like dish soap? To some degree, yes. If I can't get my horror fix from Stephen King, I can easily turn to Dean Koontz. Their books are what economists call "substitute goods." If I can't get Coca-Cola, I'm happy to drink Pepsi. If I can't use Dawn to wash my dishes, I'm happy to use Dove. Advertisers are aware of this, which is why they spend so much money promoting Coke over Pepsi (and vice versa). Other than the emotional appeal used in marketing, there's not a lot of difference.

The same is true of many genre books, like romance, westerns, and science fiction. I'm usually just as happy to read Ursula K. Le Guin as I am to read Gene Wolfe. But there are exceptions. To me, Wolfe's *There Are Doors* is more than just a science-fiction entertainment. Philip K. Dick's *Do Androids Dream of Electric Sheep* speaks to me on a level that few other books attain. And what do we do when a masterpiece like *Moby Dick* comes along—or *The Adventures of Huckleberry Finn, Zen and the Art of Motorcycle Maintenance, The Mouse and His Child*? Don't you have a handful of books that have changed your life? I know I do. Such books truly are candles, and their glow illuminates the world in ways nothing else can.

Deadlines

A typesetter impatiently asked the Pen master, "When will our esteemed designer finally reach enlightenment?"

The master looked up from reviewing the publishing schedule. "She's waiting on the editor."

"And when will the editor reach enlightenment?"

"He's waiting on the designer."

Sometimes I wonder how anything gets done at all. When I worked at a trade house, I took great care to meet my deadlines, and I sometimes had to remind others that the publishing schedule belonged to everyone, not just the scheduler. Who owns the schedule? You do, whether you created it or not. Who is responsible to get a project out on time? You are, and part of that responsibility is helping others meet *their* deadlines. We're all in this together; casting blame is counterproductive. "But I have no influence over the work of others!" you say. Are you sure? Have you tried negotiating? Have you tried bribery with brownies? Have you explored ways to make your own work more efficient so that others have more time for theirs? Instead of passing the buck, see what you can do to improve the situation. (See *Influence: The Psychology of Persuasion,* by Robert B. Cialdini.) There is hidden wisdom in this famous Zen story:

> Nansen saw the monks of the eastern and western halls fighting over a cat. He seized the cat and told the monks: "If any of you say a good word, a word of Zen, you can save the cat."
>
> No one answered. So Nansen boldly cut the cat in two pieces.
>
> That evening Joshu returned and Nansen told him about this. Joshu removed his sandals and, placing them on his head, walked out.
>
> Nansen said: "If you had been there, you could have saved the cat."

The story is not about the cat, just as "Joshu's Mu" is not about the dog. Zen stories are always about *you.* Can you save the cat?

The Pen master's assistant asked an editor how long it would take to finish the manuscript on which she was working. "I should be finished tomorrow," the editor replied.

"I think that's unrealistic," the assistant said. "Really, how long do you think will it take?"

The editor consulted her schedule. "There are still some sources I need to check, and I need to make sure the chapter titles are consistently worded—stuff like that. Maybe by the end of the week."

"Okay. But you know, this is an important book. A lot is riding on it. Just do the best you can, and let me know when it's finished."

A month later, the assistant came to the office early in the morning. When he looked into the editor's cubicle, he discovered the editor asleep at her computer. She had been working on the book all night.

The quest for perfection must always be tempered by the imposition of deadlines, for nothing will ever really be perfect, and without deadlines, some projects can go on forever. As scholar and public administrator C. Northcote Parkinson wrote, "Work expands so as to fill the time available for its completion." (*The Economist*, November 19, 1955.) Sometimes, getting something done is more important than getting it right—unpleasant for us picky editors to contemplate, but true nonetheless.

Efficiency

One day a messenger from Accounting came to see the Pen master, saying, "The Corporate overlords have decreed that we must measure the efficiency of the editing staff."

"I see," said the master. "And how do you propose to do that?"

"By counting the number of errors still remaining in each printed book."

"Very well," said the master. "We will begin hiring additional editing staff immediately."

"I don't understand," said the messenger. "That will lessen efficiency, not improve it."

"True," said the master. "But who else will look for errors in the printed books?"

The famous management consultant W. Edwards Deming is often quoted as saying "If you can't measure it, you can't manage it." What he actually said is this: "It is wrong to suppose that if you can't measure it, you can't manage it—a costly myth." (*The New Economics* [Cambridge, MA: MIT Press, 2000], 35.)

The value of some activities can't be measured. How shall we count the thousands of possible changes that the editor deemed unnecessary? How do we measure the improved clarity of an edited text? How can we detect the application of the general or even specialized knowledge that a good editor needs to have?

When the messenger from Accounting came again, he told the Pen master, "The Corporate overlords have heeded your counsel. Rather than counting errors, we will simply count the number of words you edit per hour."

"I see," said the master. "But tell me: How many numbers do you crunch per hour?"

The messenger sputtered, "We in Accounting are not judged by such measures; our job is simply to make sense of the mass of data that has been entrusted to our care."

"And so it is with editing," the master replied.

The messenger considered. Then he made a deep bow.

Perfection

An author brought her manuscript to the Pen master. "This new book is my masterpiece," she said. "It needs no editing at all; it is perfect just as it is."

"Truly the book in your mind is perfect," said the master. "But this is not the book in your mind."

The job of an editor is to capture perfectly what an author *means* to say and convey that meaning intact into the mind of the reader. This, of course, is impossible in reality, but that doesn't keep us from trying, and sometimes we may come close. As the Zen masters say, "Practice itself is enlightenment."

Subhuti was Buddha's disciple. He was able to understand the potency of emptiness, the viewpoint that nothing exists except in its relationship of subjectivity and objectivity.

One day Subhuti, in a mood of sublime emptiness, was sitting under a tree. Flowers began to fall about him.

"We are praising you for your discourse on emptiness," the gods whispered to him.

"But I have not spoken of emptiness," said Subhuti.

"You have not spoken of emptiness, we have not heard emptiness," responded the gods. "This is true emptiness." And blossoms showered upon Subhuti as rain. (Paul Reps and Nyogen Senzaki, comps., *Zen Flesh, Zen Bones* [Boston: Tuttle Publishing, 1985], 53.)

Legacy

After the Pen master had retired from his job at the publishing house, he spent much time puttering about in his garden. One beautiful fall day he was visited by a former assistant.

"What a lovely garden!" the assistant said.

"Thank you," said the master, "but the garden requires constant care." He picked a dandelion that had gone to seed, then blew the tiny seedlings into the air. "Scattered to the wind," he said. "Such is the meaning of my life."

When the assistant returned to the office, she reported to the director of publishing. "I'm worried about our old master," she said. "He blew dandelion seeds into the air and said that was the meaning of his life. Surely his contributions amount to more than that!"

The director, who knew the master well, smiled and said, "You have not understood. The master is not talking of death but of life. The seeds he has blown into the wind are the books he has sent into the world. They will take root

and grow in the minds and hearts of countless thousands.
What could be of greater worth?"

CPSIA information can be obtained
at www.ICGtesting.com
Printed in the USA
BVHW031220271119
564971BV00001B/19/P